PACKING
FOR MARS

FOR KIDS

MARY
ROACH

NORTON YOUNG READERS

An Imprint of W. W. Norton & Company

Independent Publishers Since 1923

PACKING
FOR MARS

FOR KIDS

For information about permission to reproduce selections from this book,
write to Permissions, W. W. Norton & Company, Inc.,
500 Fifth Avenue, New York, NY 10110

For information about special discounts for bulk purchases, please contact
W. W. Norton Special Sales at specialsales@wwnorton.com or 800-233-4830

Manufacturing by Versa Press
Book design by Beth Steidle
Production manager: Beth Steidle

Library of Congress Cataloging-in-Publication Data

Names: Roach, Mary, author. | Roach, Mary. Packing for Mars.
Title: Packing for Mars for kids / Mary Roach.
Description: New York, NY : Norton Young Readers, [2022] | "Adapted from
Packing for Mars: The Curious Science of Life in the Void." | Audience: Ages 9–12
Identifiers: LCCN 2021050555 | ISBN 9781324019374 (hardcover) |
ISBN 9781324019381 (epub)
Subjects: LCSH: Space biology—Juvenile literature. | Manned space flight—
Juvenile literature. | Astronauts—Training of—Juvenile literature.
Classification: LCC QH327 .R625 2022 | DDC 571.0919—dc23/eng/20211022
LC record available at https://lccn.loc.gov/2021050555

W. W. Norton & Company, Inc.
500 Fifth Avenue, New York, N.Y. 10110
www.wwnorton.com

W. W. Norton & Company Ltd.
15 Carlisle Street, London W1D 3BS

0 9 8 7 6 5 4 3 2 1

For Gus

CONTENTS

Getting ready for space: astronauts practice in a huge, 6.2-million-gallon swimming pool at the Johnson Space Center.

INTRODUCTION

To a rocket scientist, the human being is a problem. We are the most irritating pieces of machinery a rocket scientist could ever have to deal with. We need food and water and eight hours of sleep to function. Our memory is puny. We're moody and unpredictable. A circuit board or a propulsion nozzle, on the other hand, is stable and undemanding. It does not eat or panic or forget to shut the air lock, and it never complains.

But to me, the human being is the machinery that makes space exploration so interesting. We are creatures whose bodies evolved to keep us alive and thriving on a planet with air and running water and lots of gravity. In space, none of these things exist. So it's a huge challenge to figure out ways to keep astronauts alive and healthy.

Space engineers have to rethink and redesign everything that they plan to put up into space. Not just motors and fuses and rocket engines but all the simple objects we take for granted on Earth—a bed, a toilet, a shower. A pen. A saltshaker! Without gravity, the simplest human acts have to be relearned: how to cross a room, how to eat soup, how to wash your hair.

A lot of this training and redesigning happens in and around NASA's Johnson Space Center, in Houston, Texas. NASA has planes that fly in a way that creates the experience of floating weightless without gravity. They have a giant swimming pool with replicas of the International Space Station submerged in it, so that astronauts can float around in the water wearing space suits and practicing their space walks. There are replicas of space capsules and space bathrooms and a giant simulator that lets astronauts practice parking a space capsule at 17,000 miles per hour. By visiting these places and things, it's possible, in a way, to visit space without leaving Earth. And that's what we're going to do.

This device attempted to simulate walking on the moon, where gravity is only one-sixth of that on Earth, by hanging an astronaut like a puppet and having him walk sideways along a wall, so only one-sixth of his weight rested on his feet.

1

GRAVITY RULES

On June 14, 1949, a V-2 rocket launched a monkey named Albert from the New Mexico desert—the first mammal in space.

Let's say you boarded a rocket in your backyard, strapped yourself in, and launched. After you'd gone about sixty miles up, you would arrive in space. If you lived in New York City, a journey into space would be about the same distance as a journey to Hackettstown, New Jersey. Sixty miles. You don't even need a change of underwear. Yet the idea of going up into space was extremely worrisome back before anyone had ever done it. Space was the edge of the known world. The temperature out there will kill you, and there's no air to breathe.

Plus, you would no longer experience the effects of Earth's gravity. You'd be weightless. Lighter than a soap bubble. That was an alarming proposition way back in the beginning of the space exploration era. Humans evolved for life with gravity. We're built for it. No one knew what would happen to the human body without it. What if your blood didn't flow through your blood vessels the way it's supposed to? What if your nerves stopped firing or your organs stopped working?

Until there were answers to questions like these, it seemed risky to send a person up there. So, a decade before Yuri Gagarin became the first person in space, long before John Glenn and Neil Armstrong, before Ham the astrochimp and Laika the space dog, before all of them, there was Albert.

Albert was a nine-pound rhesus monkey. In 1949, dressed in a gauze diaper, little red-haired Albert, one of five spacefaring monkeys named Albert, rode a V-2 rocket into space. He was the first mammal to go there. In a history book about animals in the space program, there is a photograph of Albert just before he was loaded onto the rocket. He had been given a sedative, so his delicate eyelids are closed, like a doll's. He looks very small beside that fifty-foot rocket.

The Albert project was the first time monkeys were sent into space, but it was not the first time scientists turned to animals to calm their nerves about the medical effects of going high into the sky. The first time was 1783. The experimenters were Joseph and Étienne Montgolfier, the inventors of the hot-air balloon. The "high" altitude they were curious about, were

The Montgolfier brothers' balloon, which carried a sheep, a duck, and a rooster to an altitude of 1,500 feet in 1783.

11

worried about, was 1,500 feet. These days you can go that high just by riding an elevator to the top of some big-city skyscrapers, but to people back then it seemed impossibly, frighteningly far up.

The hot-air balloon experiment was like something from a children's book. A sheep, a duck, and a rooster went for a ride in a wicker box beneath a beautiful balloon. They soared above the king's palace and across the courtyard while the people below them cheered. After drifting for two miles, the balloon landed uneventfully. "The animals were fine," reads Étienne Montgolfier's report about the flight, "and the sheep had pissed in the cage."

Back before rockets started carrying astronauts, they carried bombs. Rather than dropping the bombs from airplanes—a dangerous job for the military crew on the plane—the bombs could be packed inside a rocket and launched far and fast into enemy lands. Launched how? By setting off a controlled explosion at the bottom of the rocket—the same way rockets are launched today. Putting an astronaut on a rocket was—and still is—a pretty risky thing to do. So it may seem strange that the thing that most worried the early space scientists was . . . gravity.

Let's talk about gravity. Just a bit. If you are like me, you have probably thought about gravity mostly in terms of minor annoyances. Plates and glasses dropped and broken. Bicycles falling over. Pants falling down. But gravity is a little more serious than that. Gravity is one of the "fundamental forces" that control the universe.

Gravity is the pull of one object on another. Its effects are most noticeable with hugely massive objects, like planets and moons and stars. Our sun is a star, and its gravitational pull keeps planet Earth traveling around it rather than flying off into the wider universe. Earth's gravity, in turn, keeps the moon hanging around. The more massive the objects and the closer they are to each other, the stronger the pull of gravity. The moon is more than two hundred thousand miles away from us, yet it is so massive that as it circles Earth, it pulls the oceans toward itself. The moon's gravity is why we have ocean tides.

Gravity is one reason there is life on Earth. Yes, we need air and water to survive. But without gravity, our atmosphere—the gas molecules that make up our air—would drift away into space along with the water in the seas and the cars on the roads and you and me and anything else that's not tied down. It is gravity that holds it all to the planet's surface.

The International Space Station circles Earth about 250 miles high. Up there, the Earth's gravitational pull is about 10 percent weaker than it is here on the planet's surface. That's not a huge difference. So why do astronauts on the space station float around as though there were no gravity at all? In truth, they are not really floating; they are falling. The station and everyone on it are constantly falling in a loop around Earth.

Here's what's going on. As a spacecraft plows through the Earth's atmosphere, it slowly loses the forward momentum it got from the launch blast. Meanwhile, Earth's gravity is pulling it back. Eventually gravity begins to win the tug-of-war. When you combine those two forces—out to space and back to Earth—the result is a curved path that loops around the Earth. That loop is called an orbit.

Either way you look at it—floating or falling— the people on the International Space Station are weightless. And the effects of weightlessness were what space scientists needed to understand. The

Albert project was the beginning of that research, but research continues today.

That same history book that had the photograph of Albert the monkey also had a picture of the printout from the device that monitored Albert's heartbeat in space. These days doctors can send email to and from space and even look at ultrasound images of injured or sick astronauts. But back in 1949, the technology was limited. You could monitor heartbeat and breathing rate, and not much else.

That wasn't enough. The scientists needed to know more. Would astronauts in space be able to swallow, or did they need gravity to help the food move along? How would they drink water? Would they still be able to empty their bladder? What if their eyeballs changed shape and their vision became blurry? If they cut themselves, would their blood still clot and scab over?

To find out the answers, scientists needed study subjects they could talk to and work with. They needed humans. If they were going to use humans, they needed a safer way to answer those questions. They needed to somehow create weightlessness without launching someone on a rocket into space.

Shortly after the Albert flight, scientists came up with a way to do that. The technique is called a parabolic flight. It works like this. A pilot flies a plane in a big arc—up, over, and back down. As the plane flies over the top of the arc and back down, those on board become weightless. They float in the air for about 20 to 30 seconds. Then, instead of landing, the pilot pulls out of the dive and heads back up and over the arc again. This roller-coaster path is repeated over and over until the fuel runs low. In this way, scientists were able to study the effects of weightlessness in half-minute chunks. If you add up all the chunks of time, each parabolic flight could provide scientists with

Two of the United States' first astronauts in simulated weightless conditions during a parabolic flight in 1959.

several minutes of weightlessness in which to run their experiments.

In 1958, fifteen volunteers from the U.S. Air Force School of Aviation Medicine boarded an F-94C fighter plane to help answer the questions space scientists had. While the subjects were floating, the researchers had them try some things. It turned out that, yes, people can swallow food without gravity's help. They can see clearly, and if they use a straw, they have no trouble drinking. To see if humans could urinate normally, the researchers made special urine collection systems out of old hoses and small weather balloons. To make sure the volunteers had to "go," they were asked to drink eight glasses of water over the two hours leading up to the flight. Two of the men were unable to hold it that long and dropped out of the test. But the rest peed into the weather balloons without a problem. All systems go for space travel!

Parabolic flights are still flown today by space agencies like NASA. These days, it's not human beings they're testing. It's equipment. Every time NASA develops a new pump or heater or toilet, the new piece of equipment is loaded onto a plane for a parabolic flight, to make sure it's going to work okay when it's weightless in space.

Until recently, a few dozen humans would go up on NASA's parabolic flights, too. While I was working on this project, I was lucky enough to be one of them. The next chapter is the story of what that was like.

Space shuttle astronauts aboard a parabolic flight in 1978.

2

WHAT IT'S LIKE TO FLY

Everything that goes into space is tested in simulated weightless conditions—including this motorcycle designed for the Apollo moon landings. It was never used.

Building 993 at Ellington Field airport has a sign outside the door. The sign says: REDUCED GRAVITY OFFICE. Unless you happen to know what goes on inside that office, it sounds pretty fabulous. It sounds like an office with laptops and coffeepots floating through the air and secretaries drifting here and there like paper airplanes.

In fact, it's just a regular office. It's the office of the people who run NASA's Reduced Gravity Student Flight Opportunities Program. Teams of college students compete for the chance to carry out experiments in a simulated weightless environment.

Each winning team is allowed to bring along a journalist to write about their project. I'm the journalist for a team from Missouri University of Science and Technology. My team is studying welding in space. Astronauts often have to assemble things and attach them to the outside or inside of their spacecraft—solar panels, or robotic arms, for example. Usually they bolt things in place rather than weld them. Sparks and melted metal make NASA nervous. A blob of superhot metal that drifts onto an astronaut's space suit could melt through all the layers and cause a leak. If a space suit loses its air pressure, the astronaut inside it is in grave danger. Also, no one was sure whether weightless welding would result in weaker welds. That's what Team Space Weld will be investigating.

The night before our flight, I pick up some Thai food and bring it back to my hotel. Because the hotel is across the street from Johnson Space Center, NASA TV is what you see when you first switch on the television. This evening, they're showing footage from the opening of a new laboratory unit that has just docked with the International Space Station. The unit—or "module"—was made by Japan's space agency, JAXA. After a floating press conference, the astronauts enter the new module for the first time and zoom around. I've watched a lot of NASA TV, and you rarely see astronauts horsing around like this. You'll see a guy hunched over a circuit board, toes hooked under a foot restraint, bobbing gently like an anchored boat. Or you see the crew talking into a press camera, holding still in two neat rows. If it weren't for the brief moments when the microphone floats or someone's necklace hovers in front of her chin, you could easily forget these humans are weightless.

But not tonight! One astronaut is spinning in the air like an actor in a martial arts movie. Another is ricocheting like a ball on a pool table—wall to ceiling to wall to floor. No one wears shoes, because no one's feet need to be on the floor. One of the Japanese astronauts is crouched at the doorway to the module, waiting for a clear path all the way across. He pushes off and flies through empty air, his arms held out in front of him like a superhero.

Tomorrow this will be me. I go to sleep feeling like I felt when I was a kid the night before Christmas.

From the outside, the plane looks like any other large jet plane. But inside, it's completely different. Most of the seats have been removed, so it's more like a workshop than an airplane. Only six rows of seats remain, way in the back. As I arrive, Team Space Weld's experiment is being loaded on board. For safety, the welding device is fixed to the floor of the plane.

After a few minor delays, it's time to fly. We buckle up and head south, to the skies over the Gulf of Mexico. It's a beautiful sunny day, but you can't really tell right now. Once we arrived at the area where the roller-coaster part begins, the window shades were all closed. This is because the plane will be flying at alarmingly steep angles up and then down toward the water. Best not to look out the window.

✦

I should be down near the floor with my team, taking notes on how the experiment is going. I can't do this, however, because my notebook is floating in the air in front of my face, with the pages all fanned out, and I want to keep looking at it for a while longer. It hovers, not rising and not falling, in the manner of a birthday balloon a few days after the party. It's the strangest, coolest thing ever.

Weightlessness feels like nothing else I've experienced. You never think about the weight of your organs inside you. Your heart is a half-pound of muscle hanging off your aorta. Your liver uses your stomach as a beanbag chair. Your arms burden your shoulders like curtains on a rod. Even the weight of your hair creates a feeling on your scalp. In weightlessness, all this

The author and her notebook, floating aboard a parabolic flight.

27

disappears. Everything weighs nothing! The result is a feeling of unimaginable lightness.

Last night on NASA TV, an astronaut told a middle-school student that being weightless feels like floating in water. It does, but it also doesn't. In water, you sense the liquid's help—making you buoyant and supporting your weight. When you move, you feel the water push back on you. You are floating, but a heaviness remains. Here on the plane, for 20 seconds at a time, you float in the air without effort, without help, without resistance.

The only things weighing me down right now are NASA's rules. We have been told to hold on to a strap with one hand at all times. This means that every time I'm floating, I reach the limits of my strap and swing around to the left. This causes me to enter the airspace over one team's electromagnetic docking experiment. To get out of their way, I have to reach my leg down and push off from the frame of their device.

"Don't kick their experiment!" barks a NASA rule enforcer in a blue flight suit. As if I meant to. *I hate your stupid electromagnetic docking thing, take that!* Of course I didn't. It's just that this floating business takes some getting used to. Yesterday at Johnson Space Center, I talked about this with an astronaut named Lee Morin. He told me it takes about a week to feel comfortable floating instead of walking. "Then it seems like the natural thing—to float," he said. "And it seems very odd to think about walking."

"Feet down!" yells another man in a blue flight suit. This is our cue to bring our legs back underneath us, because the plane is pulling out of its dive and we're starting to have weight again. It happens gradually—you don't suddenly fall to the floor—but still, you don't want to land on your head.

After 20 seconds on the floor of the plane, we start to float again. We all rise up off the floor like cartoon ghosts. Everyone's grinning and laughing. It's hard to believe, but I've heard that the thrill wears off pretty fast. "At first," wrote astronaut Michael Collins, in a book about his trip to the moon, "just floating around is great fun, but then after a while it becomes annoying, and you want to stay in one place. . . . My hands kept floating up in front of me, and I wished I had pockets or somewhere to put them."

Astronaut Andy Thomas told me how irritating it was to never be able to set something down. "Everything has to have a bit of Velcro on it," he said. "You're forever losing things. I brought one nail file with me on Mir, so I was very careful with it." Mir was a space

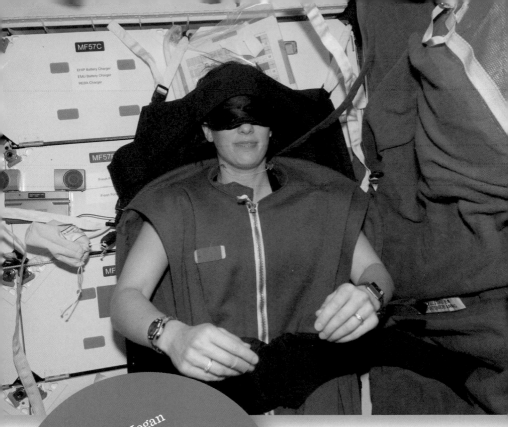

Astronaut Megan McArthur sleeping in space. Weightlessness can be annoying: another astronaut, Michael Collins, said, "My hands kept floating up in front of me, and I wished I had pockets or somewhere to put them."

station built by the Soviet Union (now Russia). "About a month before the end of the mission, it popped out of my hand. I turned to grab it, and it was just gone." One time his crewmate lost a whole box of trash. "Big thing.

Gone. We never saw it again." Aleksandr Laveikin, who also spent time on Mir, said he soon started to miss walking. "Only in space do you understand what incredible happiness it is, just to walk," he told me. "To walk on Earth."

Without gravity, things don't work quite the same as they do here on Earth. Even something as simple as a fuse. Fuses have a metal strip that melts if a dangerous amount of electricity is flowing through it. The melted metal drips away, leaving a gap that breaks the flow of electricity and cuts off the power. It's a safety device. But in weightlessness, the droplet doesn't drip, so the electricity continues to flow and things overheat and soon the equipment is fried.

Overheated equipment is a common concern with weightlessness. Anything that generates heat tends to overheat, because there are no air currents to move the heat away. Normally, hot air rises—because it's lighter than cold air—and cooler, denser, heavier air flows in to fill the empty space left behind. But in weightlessness, the hotter, lighter air stays where it is, all around the piece of equipment, getting hotter and hotter. Eventually it damages the equipment.

Human machinery tends to overheat for the same reason. The International Space Station has lots of fans to blow the heated air around. Without the fans, all the heat that comes off exercising astronauts would just hang around their body. They'd have their own personal Florida summer. Their exhaled breath would also hover around them. Astronauts who hang their sleeping sacks in a poorly ventilated place may get a carbon dioxide headache.

In the case of one member of Team Space Weld, the human machinery didn't overheat, but as we're about to see, it got pretty messed up.

On the ceiling of the plane is a lit-up number, like the kind you see at deli counters, telling customers who is being served. This one is counting the parabolas— twenty-seven so far. Three more to go. We have been told not to go "Supermanning" around, but I can't help myself. On the twenty-eighth parabola, I pull up my legs, crouch on the window, and then gently uncoil, launching myself across the cabin of the plane. It's like pushing off from the wall of a swimming pool, but the pool is empty and it's air you're gliding through.

Later, when I look at my notebook, I'll see that I've written very little about space welding. Mostly, I've written stuff like *"Wahooo!"*

It's probably the coolest afternoon of my entire life.

But not of Pat Zerkel's life. The young Missouri space welder has been safety-belted into the seats at the back of the plane. A white vomit bag hovers near his face, and he holds it open with both hands.

"*OOOooulllrr-aaghchkkk, khkkk.*" And now the bag is closed. Pat has been joyless since the fourth parabola. At parabola number twelve, the men in blue flight suits gave Pat a sedative and helped him to the back of the plane. This was done to help him feel better, but also for our benefit: if he stayed out here with the rest of us and didn't grab a vomit bag in time, gobs of his breakfast would be floating through the air for the rest of the flight.

What makes motion sickness especially cruel is that generally speaking, it strikes during life's happiest times. A sunset sail on the San Francisco Bay, a child's first roller-coaster ride, a rookie astronaut's trip to space. There are few faster routes from joy to misery, from *Wahooo* to *ooulllrr-aaghchkkk*.

For an astronaut, motion sickness is more than an unpleasant embarrassment. An entire Soviet mission, Soyuz 10, was apparently cut short due to motion sickness. An incapacitated crew member makes for the most costly sick day in the world.

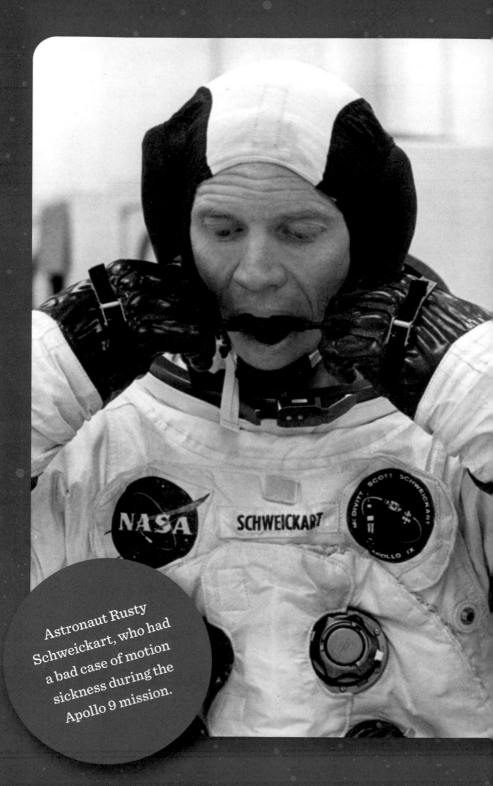

Astronaut Rusty Schweickart, who had a bad case of motion sickness during the Apollo 9 mission.

3

BARFING ON THE CEILING

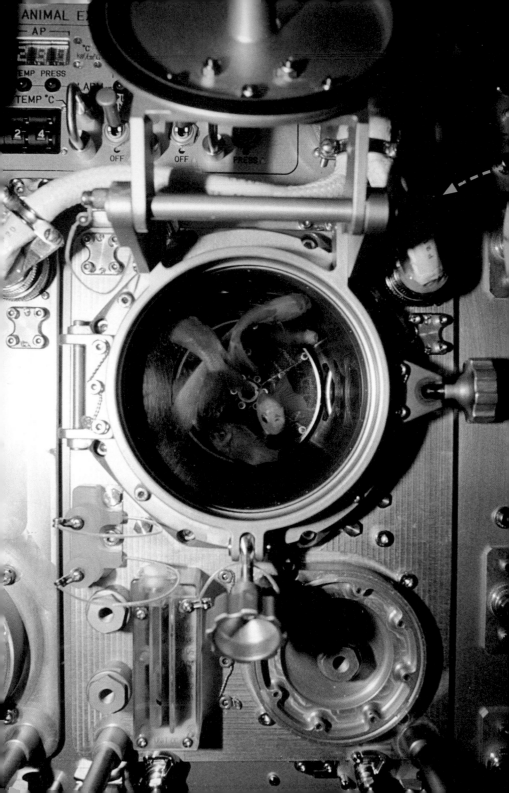

On September 12, 1962, President John F. Kennedy announced a goal of landing an American on the moon by the end of the decade. NASA's Apollo space program was created to reach that goal. The Apollo missions were named with numbers. The one most people know about is Apollo 11: on July 20, 1969, Neil Armstrong and Buzz Aldrin became the first humans to set foot on the moon.

We're going to back up a bit, to Apollo 9. It is March 1969—nine months before the end of the decade. The United States and the Soviet Union are racing neck and neck to be the first nation to put a human on the moon. On March 5, a Wednesday afternoon, 200,000 miles from Earth, an Apollo 9 astronaut named Rusty Schweickart was getting ready to leave the safety of his space capsule.

Schweickart's job on this day was to test one of the big white life-support

Fish swimming in space, in an experiment aboard Skylab. Even fish can get motion sickness.

backpacks that Neil Armstrong and Buzz Aldrin would be wearing when they walked on the moon. Without the machinery inside the backpack, Neil and Buzz would quickly suffocate and overheat. The life-support backpacks had been tested in weightlessness—on one of the parabolic flights we learned about in the last chapter—but they had never been tested in the airlessness of space.

That is what was on Schweickart's to-do list that day. It was what he trained for, and it was super-important. He would put on the life-support backpack and try it out in the airlessness and extreme temperatures of space.

There was a problem this afternoon. Rusty Schweickart was not feeling well. He had a bad case of space motion sickness. He'd been throwing up, and throwing up inside a space suit is dangerous. It's dangerous enough that Schweickart and his crewmates thought about canceling the test. Schweickart remembers thinking, "Is this basically a wasted mission because Schweickart's barfing? . . . I mean, I had a real possibility in my mind at the time of being *the* cause of missing Kennedy's challenge of going to the moon and back by the end of the decade."

What's the big deal with vomiting in your space helmet? "You die," said Schweickart. "You can't get that sticky stuff away from your mouth. . . . It just floats right there and you have no way of getting it away from your nose or your mouth so that you can breathe, and you are going to die."

Or not. Space suit engineers have given a lot of thought to this. One engineer I talked with said that NASA's helmets, including those of the Apollo missions, have air flowing down across the astronaut's face. The air blows hard enough that if you were to puke inside your helmet, the puke would be blown down away from your face and into the body of the space suit. Disgusting? Yes. Fatal? No. You can bet that the helmet and air system were carefully tested on a parabolic flight.

Even if a gob of vomit hovered and clung to your nose and mouth, you would still be unlikely to die. Because if you were to breathe in your vomit—or, for that matter, anyone else's—it triggers a protective reflex: you cough. The cough would blow the vomit back out of your airway.

That's good, because vomit is a more dangerous thing to inhale than water. Vomit comes up from the stomach, and the stomach contains acid and digestive enzymes. So inhaled vomit could burn or damage the inside of your lungs. Imagine what would happen if vomit got in your eyes. "Barf bouncing off the helmet and back into the eyes would be really debilitating," said the space suit engineer I spoke to. That's the thing that's actually really dangerous about throwing up inside a space helmet. You'd be temporarily blinded.

Even if the vomit didn't get in your eyes, it might stick to your helmet visor—the part the astronaut looks through. That would of course also make it dangerously hard to see. Something similar happened during Apollo 16. It wasn't vomit, though. It was orange-flavored Tang, an artificial drink. Astronaut Charlie Duke's in-suit drink bag had begun leaking on the moon. (In-suit drink bags were like the CamelBak water bags people use today while hiking.) Blobs of liquid Tang were floating in front of Duke's face and clinging to his helmet visor. "I tell you, it's pretty hard to see things when you've got a helmet full of orange juice," Duke said. Here he is in the Apollo 16 mission transcript, talking to Mission Control while he was out and about on the moon. A pair of craters—named Wreck and Trap—have just come into view. "I can see Wreck and Trap and orange juice."

In the history of the space program, only one astronaut has upchucked while wearing a space helmet. It was smelly and unpleasant but not dangerous, because very little came up. It happened in the airlock of the International Space Station. The space motion sickness researcher who told me about it did not share the astronaut's name. Even today, having motion sickness in space is something astronauts prefer to keep to themselves.

This was especially true back in Rusty Schweickart's day. The attitude during Apollo, he recalls, was that "motion sickness is something that weenies suffer." Astronaut Gene Cernan agreed: "To admit being sick was to admit a weakness, not only to the public and the other [astronauts] but also to the doctors . . ." And if the doctors knew you were prone to getting motion sickness, you might not be chosen for any more missions. Schweickart never went up in space again.

Motion sickness hits some people faster and harder than it hits others, but almost nobody is immune. If the conditions are rough enough, nearly everyone will barf. Even fish can get seasick.

In reality, somewhere between half and three-quarters of all astronauts have reported that they suffered from space motion sickness. That's why you don't always see many news interviews the first day or two of a mission. The astronauts are probably off in a corner somewhere, throwing up. A lot of first-time astronauts think they'll be fine, but they're often wrong. Luckily, launch pad workers know this. They stuff extra vomit bags in the pockets of rookie astronauts' pressure suits before liftoff.

After astronauts finally adjust to being weightless, they have to readjust when they come back down to Earth. Instead of space motion sickness, now they have Earth motion sickness. (It's also called landing vertigo.) And that's why astronauts don't go on TV right after they come back down to Earth. Because they can't walk without falling down. They're dizzy and nauseous. Plus they're trying to relearn how to use their legs!

After he came home from Apollo 9, Schweickart dedicated himself to the study of motion sickness. "I became the guinea pig, the pincushion that people stuck their pins in and their probes and whatnot. For six months . . . my main job was learning as much as we could about motion sickness."

To figure out the best ways to prevent motion sickness, you first need to figure out the best ways to cause it. Researchers at the U.S. Naval Aerospace Medical

Institute, in Pensacola, Florida, were very good at that. They were the inventors of the human disorientation device. Picture a chicken turning on a rotisserie spit. But instead of a chicken, it's a research subject harnessed to a chair. The chair and the person in it are turning—up to thirty times per minute. (By comparison, a chicken on a motorized spit typically rotates just five times per minute.) It wasn't easy to find volunteers for this. In one experiment, more than half of the volunteers quit before it ended.

A volunteer prepares for a test in the human disorientation device.

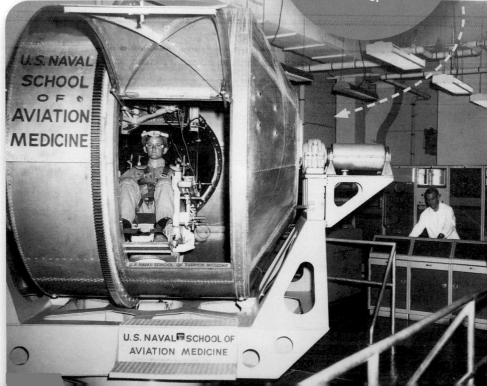

U.S. NAVAL SCHOOL OF AVIATION MEDICINE

U.S. NAVAL SCHOOL OF AVIATION MEDICINE

NASA astronaut Jack Fischer gets ready for his mission aboard the International Space Station by taking a ride on a rotating chair to test his vestibular system.

These days, motion sickness researchers use a device called the rotating chair. This chair is upright, like a normal chair, but it has a small motor at the base that makes it spin. The study subjects are asked to sit in the chair and close their eyes. After they've been spinning for a few moments, the experimenter tells them to tilt their head—to the left and then to the right, over and over while they spin. I took a ride on the rotating chair at the lab of a NASA space motion sickness researcher named Pat Cowings. At the very first head tilt, my guts lurched inside me. It was awful. "I can make a rock sick," said Dr. Cowings, and I believe her.

What has science learned from all this? For starters, we know what causes motion sickness: something called "sensory conflict." That is, your eyes are telling your brain something other than what your vestibular system is telling it.

Say you are a passenger on a boat on a stormy day. You are down below the deck, in a room with no windows. Since the walls and floor are moving along with you, your eyes tell your brain that you are sitting still. But your inner ear tells a different story. As the ship moves you up and down and all around, tiny calcium pebbles in your inner ear—called otoliths—

are also moving around. This is your vestibular system telling your brain—correctly—that you are moving. So your brain gets confused. It responds to the confusion by making you feel nauseous.

Weightlessness creates worse sensory conflict than seasickness. On Earth, when you're standing or sitting upright, the little pebbles, or otoliths, come to rest on the bottom of a chamber in the inner ear. When, say, you lie down on your side, they come to rest on the side of that chamber. But when you're weightless, the otoliths just float around in the middle of the chamber, regardless of whether the astronaut is upright or lying down. Now if she suddenly moves her head, the pebbles ricochet back and forth. So her inner ear says she just lay down and stood up and lay down and stood up. Meanwhile her eyes are saying she simply turned her head. Until her brain learns to reinterpret the conflicting information, she's likely to feel pretty crummy.

For the first few days of a space mission, astronauts are advised to avoid doing flips in the air and other things that, while fun, cause their otoliths to bounce around inside their ears. In one space experiment, a researcher attached a motion sensor to the heads of a crew of astronauts. The astronauts who tended to move their heads around a lot were the ones who suffered the most from motion sickness. What's true in space is true in a car on a winding road: no matter how much the driver behind you looks like Jabba the Hutt, don't whip your head around to look.

That same researcher suggested that astronauts could wear caps that were wired to beep if they moved their head too fast or too much. The idea was to help them be more aware of their movements. Somebody—I'm guessing the astronauts—nixed the beeping beanies.

The early astronauts on space stations had to deal with an especially intense sensory conflict. It was called the visual reorientation illusion. They'd be working on something and suddenly their sense of "up" would flip to "down." It happened most often in modules that had no obvious clues as to which was the floor and which was the ceiling or the wall. "You were working on a task . . . and . . . then turning away and finding that the whole room was completely cattywampus to what you thought it was," recalls a Spacelab astronaut. Another problem was that different modules were set up differently. One might have the lights on the "ceiling," and the one attached to it would have lights on the "floor." So when astronauts floated from one module into the other, it could make them feel disoriented and nauseous.

Sometimes it was a fellow astronaut who caused this sort of thing. Several Spacelab astronauts described "sudden vomiting episodes" after looking up and seeing a crewmember upside down.

Hanging around upside down is a problem for another reason. Astronaut Lee Morin told me it's hard to understand what someone is saying when his mouth is upside down. When we talk with someone, we read that person's lips more than we realize. Plus, he added, "You get the chin thing." Where the person's chin looks like her nose. Creepy.

In space, as at sea, feeling better takes time. Getting over motion sickness is a process of adaptation—of giving your brain time to adjust to the new reality. That's why astronauts on longer

Sometimes just seeing another crew member upside down can cause an attack of vomiting. Astronauts Eugene Cernan and Ronald Evans during Apollo 17.

missions are often discouraged from taking motion sickness medications. The drugs will just delay their adaptation. They'll have to go through it eventually. Of course, for anyone taking a short trip, say a whale-watching cruise or a parabolic flight, motion sickness drugs are extremely helpful. I would have been puking right along with Pat Zerkel if I hadn't taken my pill.

Another thing the researchers learned is that it helps to focus on something other than how sick you

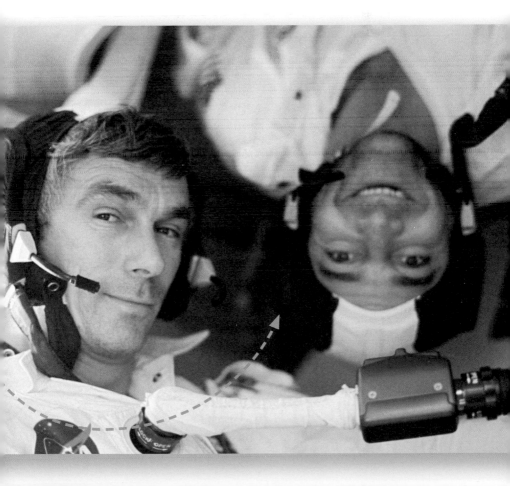

feel. Remember the people rotisserating on the human disorientation device? The ones who suffered the least were the ones who had been given math questions to do in their heads. Distraction is good medicine.

For Rusty Schweickart on Apollo 9, everything went wrong. Because he'd been sick during parabolic training flights down on Earth, he tried to keep his head very still once he got to space. That delayed his adaptation—problem number one. By day three, the day of the life-support backpack test, his crewmates had already adapted to weightlessness. But Schweickart had not.

As part of the test, Schweickart had to put on his space suit. That's a complicated maneuver that involves a lot of ducking down and bending over. That was problem number two: extreme and sudden head movements. "Suddenly I had to barf . . . and I mean, that's not a good feeling. But of course you feel better after you barf." Encouraged, he continued his preparations, moving over to a part of the spacecraft that was oriented differently from the module where he had been suiting up. "You're used to being up, and when you go over there, it's down." Problem number

One astronaut holds another upside down using just one finger aboard Skylab.

three: the visual reorientation illusion. He quickly felt worse.

Meanwhile, his crewmates were busy with other tasks. So Schweickart had to sit and wait, feeling sick and having nothing to distract him from those feelings—problem number four. "All of a sudden I had to barf again."

When you throw up in space, the unwritten rule is that you clean it up yourself. Though Schweickart's fellow astronauts were certainly nice about it. Here is that moment, from the mission transcript of Apollo 9:

> **Command Module Pilot Dave Scott:**
> Why don't you let all the rest of the
> powering down stuff and all that be
> ours, and you go get your suit off, clean
> up, try to eat, and go to bed?

> **Schweickart:** Okay. Cleaning up
> sounds pretty good.

> **Scott:** Get one of those towels and
> wash and . . . all that stuff. That'll make
> you feel better.

> **Schweickart:** Okay.

You might be picturing Schweickart going off to a bathroom to get cleaned up. But the early space capsules were far too small to have a bathroom. They didn't even have a toilet. As we're about to see, this was quite a challenge for NASA—and for the astronauts.

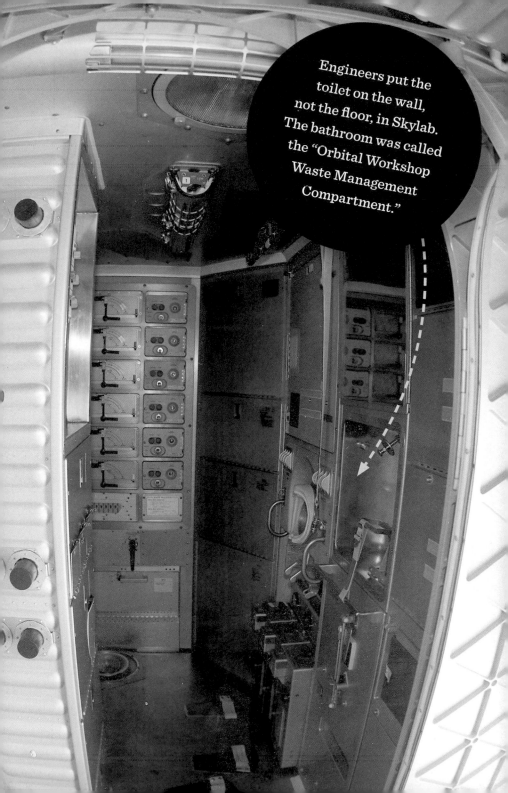

Engineers put the toilet on the wall, not the floor, in Skylab. The bathroom was called the "Orbital Workshop Waste Management Compartment."

4

TOILET TRAINING FOR GROWN-UPS

The
fecal
bag.

Gravity is good to have around. This is especially true in the bathroom. Your toilet depends on gravity. When you flush, water flows down from the toilet tank, swooshes around the toilet bowl, and goes down into the pipes and out to the sewer. Without gravity, none of that can happen. The water in the tank would stay there. Blobs of water in a toilet bowl would float up out of it.

NASA had to figure out something different. The Apollo astronauts who would be going to the moon would be up there for two weeks. They couldn't just hold it. And you couldn't ask the astronauts to poop in a plastic bag and then close it up like a bag of dog doo.

Or could you? One of the early human waste-disposal systems under consideration during the Apollo program was called the "defecation glove." The astronaut would pull a loose plastic glove on to one hand and then reach around and "go" into his palm. And then, like a dog owner using a plastic bag to pick up after the dog, he'd pull the open end down over his hand and tie off the bag.

This system was not chosen. What was chosen instead was not a whole lot more dignified. It was called the "fecal bag." Fecal, as in feces. As in poop. Bag, as in plastic bag. The fecal bag was similar to an airplane vomit bag in terms of its size and how much it could hold and how badly one did not want to have to use it. Up at the opening of the bag was a peel-and-stick ring. This was used to attach the bag to the astronaut's butt cheeks.

Weightlessness made the experience worse than it already sounds. When you use an Earth toilet, gravity causes your turd to hang heavier and heavier as more of it emerges from your body. Within seconds, it's heavy enough to pull free and drop down into the toilet bowl. Space toilet scientists call this moment "separation." Without gravity, there's no natural separation. The turd—which some NASA waste-disposal engineers politely call "the material"—just hovers there. Right where it came out. This made it impossible to close up the bag and seal it.

So the astronauts had to make separation happen by hand. They had to use their finger to coax the feces deeper into the bag, away from the opening. Thankfully, the fecal bag had a small pocket shaped like the finger of a glove. So the astronaut could stick a finger inside and do what he needed to do without his skin touching the contents of the bag.

As you might imagine, the fecal bag was not a popular item. Here is the feedback the Gemini and Apollo astronauts gave NASA:

> The fecal bag system was marginally functional and was described as very "distasteful" by the crew. The bag was considered difficult to position. Defecation was difficult to perform without the crew soiling themselves, clothing, and the cabin. The bags provided no odor control in the small capsule and the odor was prominent. Due to the difficulty of use, up to 45 minutes per defecation was required by each crew member, causing fecal odors to be present for substantial portions of the crew's day. Dislike of the fecal bags was so great that some crew continued to use . . . medication to minimize defecation during the mission.

No matter how careful the astronauts tried to be, there was occasionally an "escapee." That's the term NASA used for any bits that escaped the fecal bag before the astronaut could get it shut. Here is an excerpt from the Apollo 10 mission transcript, starring Mission Commander Thomas Stafford and Lunar Module Pilot Gene Cernan, orbiting the moon 200,000 miles from the nearest bathroom.

> **Cernan:** You know once you get out of lunar orbit, you can do a lot of things. You can power down . . . and—
>
> **Stafford [interrupting him]:** Oh—who did it?
>
> **Cernan:** What?
>
> **Stafford:** Give me a napkin quick. There's a turd floating through the air.

As soon as there were spaceships big enough to fit a toilet, the NASA engineers got to work. Instead of flushing with water—which requires gravity—they used air. The air would flow from holes under the seat and move the astronaut's "contributions" away from their butt and down into the toilet. ("Contributions" is another polite NASA bathroom word.)

Even then, there was an occasional escapee. The culprit was what the toilet engineers called "fecal popcorning." If the airflow was too strong, the poop would bounce around and bits could break off and whirl around like popcorn in an air popper. And without gravity, these bits sometimes floated up and out of the toilet. Some astronauts used the mirror in their personal hygiene kit to take a look behind themselves as they floated away from the toilet, to be sure nothing was escaping.

With the toilet on NASA's space shuttle, there was another worry: "fecal decapitation"—another technical term! The shuttle toilet had a sliding door at the top. If an astronaut were to press the button to shut the sliding door just as a piece of turd was floating up and out, the sliding door could slice off the top of it.

That made for an unfortunate situation. Because any material on the top side of the sliding door would stink up the spacecraft. And anything smeared on the underside could freeze shut the sliding door. Then the toilet would be out of order, and everyone would have to use the emergency backup system: the dreaded fecal bag. If you were the person responsible, you weren't going to be very popular with your crewmates for a while.

The first space shuttle toilet also featured a set

of whirling blades inside—like a blender. The blades would puree the waste and fling it to the sides of the holding tank, where it would stick—or was supposed to stick. Up in space, they discovered that when the material was frozen, it didn't stick as well as it should. So when the next astronaut switched on the toilet, tiny bits of frozen feces would get batted around by the blender blades. This created "fecal dust" that could float around the bathroom and result in "an unhealthy growth of *E. coli* bacteria in the mouth."

Here's how bad it got, as reported in NASA Contractor Report 3943: " . . . clouds of fecal dust generated by the zero gravity toilet have caused some astronauts to stop eating in order that they reduce their needs to use the facility." One of them even chose to use . . . the dreaded fecal bag. That's pretty bad.

The toilet on the space shuttle was a complicated machine. There were more than a dozen steps you had to take before you left the bathroom. It was so complicated that the astronauts had to go through a day of training in a replica of the shuttle bathroom that was built at Johnson Space Center. The astronauts were potty-trained!

In addition to the replica of the space shuttle toilet, the training bathroom had a second toilet. We need to talk about this one.

Imagine there was a webcam at the bottom of your toilet. Imagine that the video camera was pointing upward. At you. Very specifically, at your butt. That's what this toilet had. They called it the "potty cam." I'm pretty sure it's the only one in the world. Fortunately, only one person at a time could watch what was happening on the NASA potty cam. That person was the person who happened to be sitting on the toilet. The viewing screen was mounted right there on the wall beside the toilet.

On that same wall was a small plastic sign explaining what the toilet was made for, and how to use it. The sign said:

POSITIONAL TRAINER
Sit down on trainer seat and spread buttocks

The position and angle of an astronaut's anus as he sits on a space toilet is important. For one thing, the toilet seat is very small. Some are only five or six inches wide, as opposed to the eighteen-inch opening on a regular Earth toilet seat. The potty cam enabled the astronaut to see if his anus was centered and pointed in the right direction. If he was parked off to one side or his aim was off, he might mess up one of the air-flow holes around the toilet. If you "go" crooked and plug some of the air holes, you could disable the toilet. And it would then be *your* responsibility to clean the holes out.

The camera was helpful because without gravity, it's hard to know how your butt is positioned. You can't feel it very well, because you aren't putting your weight onto the seat. In space you have no weight. You are not so much sitting on the seat as hovering just above it.

The human body works differently in weight-lessness. The simple act of peeing can, without gravity, become a minor medical emergency. The "urge to go" is different in space. The body's early warning system doesn't work as well as it does down on Earth.

Here's why. When you're standing or sitting

on Earth, gravity pulls the urine down toward the bottom of your bladder. As your bladder fills with pee and expands, the walls stretch out. This causes special cells called "stretch receptors" to send a signal to your brain. The brain creates a feeling that tells you your bladder is getting full. As more urine accumulates, the feeling becomes stronger.

But without gravity, the urine doesn't collect on the bottom of the bladder. It floats all over the inside of the bladder. So the sides don't begin to stretch and trigger the urge to go until the bladder is almost full. By then, there may be so much urine inside that the exit tube—the urethra—is pressed shut. If that were to happen, the astronaut would need to insert a medical tube up his urethra to let out the urine. For this reason, astronauts would schedule regular toilet visits even if they didn't feel the urge to go.

✦

Like every new piece of equipment that's headed to space, a toilet must be tested to make sure it's going to work well without gravity. That means loading it onto a plane for a parabolic flight.

In the case of a toilet, the testing poses unique challenges. In order to test it, someone has to use it. And you can't schedule a BM for a certain time of day—say, when a parabolic flight is scheduled to depart. You go when you gotta go. Imagine trying to go, on command, in the space of only 20 or 30 seconds of weightlessness. I talked to a NASA scientist who was once on board with a group of engineers who were testing a space toilet. I asked him to describe the scene. He recalled that the toilet had a partial screen set up around it, but he could hear what was going on behind the screen. There was a lot of joking and people shouting words of encouragement. Lots of "Go, go, go, go!" The man failed to go. He couldn't produce.

And that explains why a team of engineers at NASA developed a "human fecal simulant"—artificial feces to plop in the toilet instead of the real deal. Of course, NASA was not the first to need such a thing. The diaper industry has used fecal simulants in order to test their products. They have gone about it in a less scientific way. They've used things that already exist. Brownie mix, peanut butter, pumpkin pie filling, and refried beans—these have all been used.

The NASA fecal simulant had to be more scien-

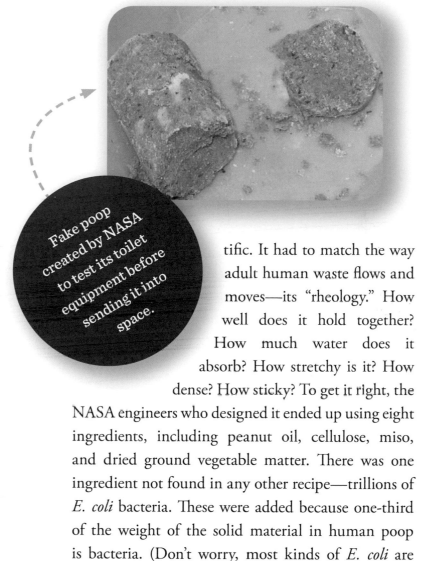

Fake poop created by NASA to test its toilet equipment before sending it into space.

tific. It had to match the way adult human waste flows and moves—its "rheology." How well does it hold together? How much water does it absorb? How stretchy is it? How dense? How sticky? To get it right, the NASA engineers who designed it ended up using eight ingredients, including peanut oil, cellulose, miso, and dried ground vegetable matter. There was one ingredient not found in any other recipe—trillions of *E. coli* bacteria. These were added because one-third of the weight of the solid material in human poop is bacteria. (Don't worry, most kinds of *E. coli* are harmless as long as they stay in your gut.)

A patch worn by NASA toilet engineers: PROUD TO BE OF SERVICE.

The engineers who developed the toilet for the space shuttle have a patch that some of them sewed onto their shirts. The design of the patch includes an image of the spacecraft, arranged inside an oval toilet seat. The slogan on the patch reads: PROUD TO BE OF SERVICE.

These men and women have good reason to be proud. To design a good space toilet you need to understand both engineering and the human body.

You can tell how important it is by what happens when it doesn't work. No other OUT OF ORDER sign can ruin a person's day as soundly as one on the door of a space bathroom. At the end of the Apollo moon exploration program, the astronauts made their feelings clear. *When you build a space station,* they said to NASA, *you had better build a toilet. No more fecal bags!*

NASA's first zero-gravity toilet was built for Skylab, an early space station. It was mounted on the wall, because that's where the designers could fit it. And when you're weightless, sitting or standing on the floor feels the same as sitting or standing on the wall or the ceiling. Up is down, and down is up. So nobody thought it would be a problem. But the astronauts didn't want to poop on a wall. They wanted their home in space to feel at least a little bit like their home on Earth.

They felt this way about the kitchen, too. The early space labs had no kitchen table, because tables make no sense without gravity. You can't put anything on them and expect it to stay there without Velcro or straps. Nonetheless, the astronauts wanted a table. At the end of their day, astronauts want to sit around a table to eat and talk and feel human and forget for a

moment that they're hurtling alone through the blackness of a very strange place far from home. When you are in a very unfamiliar place, a little familiarity can be very comforting. To this day, space stations where astronauts will be living for long stretches of time have kitchen tables (with Velcro or straps).

As for the food on that table, it looks a lot like food you could find back on Earth. But that wasn't always the case.

Astronauts sitting around the table for a meal on board the International Space Station.

71

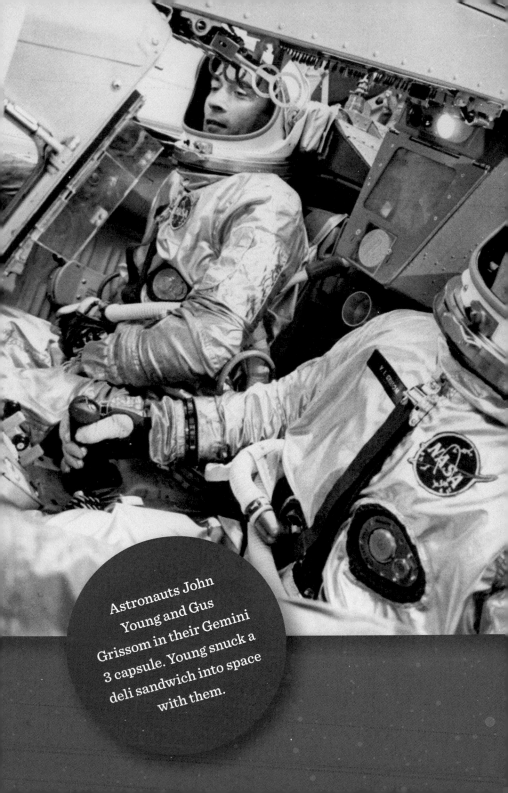

Astronauts John Young and Gus Grissom in their Gemini 3 capsule. Young snuck a deli sandwich into space with them.

5

STRANGE DINNERS

DATE FRUIT CAKE

BEEF SANDWICHES

CHEESE SANDWICHES

STRAWBERRY CUBES

Dried cube food prepared for the Apollo moon landings.

On March 23, 1965, a corned beef sandwich was launched into space. The sandwich came from Wolfie's deli in Cocoa Beach, Florida, close to Kennedy Space Center. Astronaut John Young broke a lot of rules and smuggled it on board the space capsule to surprise his crewmate, astronaut Gus Grissom. Grissom was surprised, but he didn't laugh. Here is the sandwich moment as it's recorded in the Gemini 3 mission transcript, about two hours into the flight:

Grissom: Where did that come from?

Young: I brought it with me. Let's see how it tastes. Smells, doesn't it?

Grissom: Yes, [and] it's breaking up. I'm going to stick it in my pocket.

Young: It was a thought, anyway.

Grissom: Yep.

Everything about that sandwich was wrong for space. Food to eat in a space capsule had to be pretty much the opposite of a Wolfie's deli sandwich. For one thing, it needs to be lightweight. The more a space capsule weighs, the harder it is to blast it up into space. And the more fuel it takes to get it up there. Every extra pound of weight costs thousands of dollars in extra rocket fuel. So that was a super-expensive corned beef sandwich.

Space food also needs to be small, because space capsules have very little storage room. The whole interior of the Gemini space capsule was no bigger than the inside of a two-seat sports car. Because of these limits on size and weight, NASA tried to make space foods that packed a lot of calories and vitamins into every bite.

Bacon was a good choice for space food, because it has lots of fat and protein. To make the bacon smaller, food scientists used a machine called a hydraulic press to squeeze it into a tiny square. They called it, naturally, the bacon square.

Compressed—or squeezed—food was also less likely to crumble and shed crumbs. That's important inside a spacecraft, because crumbs can be a hazard. Without gravity, a crumb does not drop to the floor.

Like everything else in space, it floats. So a crumb could easily drift behind a control panel and mess up the electronics. That's why Grissom quickly stashed the deli sandwich in his pocket when he saw that it was falling apart.

Unlike a Wolfie's sandwich, NASA food cubes could be eaten in one bite. Even a piece of toast will drop no crumbs if you are able to pop the whole thing into your mouth at once. A typical breakfast for the Gemini and Apollo astronauts was egg bites, bacon squares, and toasted bread cubes. Instead of butter, the toast cubes had a thick coating of lard to prevent crumbs from flaking off.

NASA made sandwiches, too. They called them "sandwich bites." The NASA bite-sized sandwiches had a long list of manufacturing requirements. Each sandwich bite had to weigh 3.1 grams or less. It could not "break apart when handled." It could have no "damp or soggy areas" and no "rancid" odors. The Wolfie's sandwich would have failed all these requirements. It was a great big mess, and Young got into a load of trouble because of it.

But you could understand why he did it. NASA's food cubes and "bites" were compact and tidy but not very appealing. You can get a feeling for what they were like by reading the actual NASA recipes, which have directions like this: "Chill fat-coated toast pieces until they congeal . . ." Picture some bacon grease in the bottom of a pan that's been left out overnight. That's congealed fat. You could see what the astronauts themselves had to say about their congealed fat-coated food by reading the mission transcripts. Here is astronaut Jim Lovell, complaining to Mission Control during Gemini 7: "Leaves a bad taste in your mouth and a coating on the roof of your mouth."

There was another reason the astronauts didn't like the early space foods. Cube foods were strange. They didn't seem like food. When you're hurtling through space in a cold, cramped metal capsule, you want to have something comforting and familiar for dinner. Freeze-dried "astronaut ice cream" appeals to tourists in NASA gift shops because it's a novelty, but astronauts flying around in space had all the novelty they could stand. (Freeze-dried ice cream went up into space only once. The astronauts did not enjoy it.)

The early space explorers missed and craved fresh food. The diary of Valentin Lebedev, a Russian cosmonaut on the Soviet space station Salyut 7, includes a story about a batch of onion bulbs sent up to the spacecraft for a study about how plants grow in weightlessness. "As we were unloading the re-supply ship, we found some rye bread," he wrote. "Then we saw the onion bulbs we were supposed to plant. We ate them right then and there, with bread and salt. They were delicious. Time went by and the biologists asked us, 'How are the onions?' . . . We asked to speak to the head biologist in private. 'For God's sake,' we told him, 'don't get upset. We ate your onions.'"

Here's something else that was strange about NASA's space food cubes. They were dehydrated—the water had been removed to make them lighter. They were so dry that in order to swallow them, the astronauts had to first moisten them with their saliva to replace the missing water. They had to hold the cubes in their mouth for 10 seconds to make them moist enough to hold together after they were chewed.

The very first space meals were made during the Mercury program, which began in the late 1950s. These meals came in tubes about the size of toothpaste tubes, which the astronauts would squeeze, shooting the food directly into their mouths. That way, there were no crumbs or drips to float around the spacecraft and cause problems. I tried one of the tube meals. (They are still made today, for fighter jet pilots, who attach stiff straws to them and squeeze them through openings in their helmets.) The label on the tube said Sloppy Joe, but it was nothing like eating a Sloppy Joe. It wasn't sloppy, there was no bun, and there were no chunks of ground beef. Everything had been thrown in a blender and pureed. It was like sucking down pizza sauce for dinner.

The Mercury astronauts didn't like the tube foods because they couldn't see or smell their food before they ate it. Dinner is something you experience with your eyes and nose, not just your mouth. So the Mercury

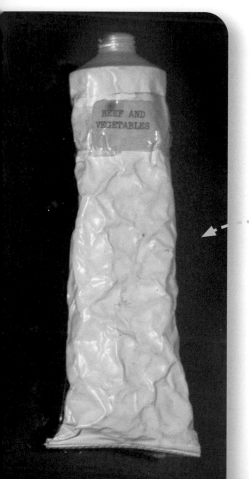

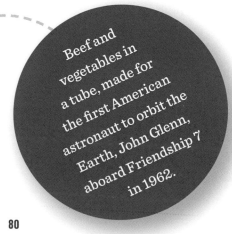

Beef and vegetables in a tube, made for the first American astronaut to orbit the Earth, John Glenn, aboard Friendship 7 in 1962.

astronauts mostly just skipped meals. This wasn't a problem, because those very first trips into space were shorter than a day.

Most of the Gemini missions were also pretty short. You can get by without eating much for a couple of days, and that's what some of the Gemini astronauts did. On mission after mission, the little food cubes would fly up into space, circle the Earth a few times, and come back down. Uneaten.

There was another reason the Gemini astronauts preferred not to eat during their space flights. If you didn't eat, you might not need to poop. That was a good thing, because, remember, there were no toilets in the early space capsules. There were just . . . the dreaded fecal bags. "On the short missions of Mercury and Gemini," wrote astronaut Frank Borman, in a book about his time in space, "a bowel movement was rare."

Gemini 7 was the exception. It was two weeks long. Borman and his crewmate, Jim Lovell, tried to go the whole time without pooping. Borman almost made it. "Frank went, I think, nine days without having to go to the bathroom," said Lovell during an interview with a NASA historian (he meant number two). On the ninth day, Borman turned to Lovell

with a grim look on his face
and said, "Jim, this is it."

Soon after Gemini 7,
NASA would be sending
astronauts to the moon. A
trip to the moon and back
could last as long as two weeks.
Refusing to eat was not an option.
What the astronauts really wanted was
a pill with all the vitamins and nutrients they
needed, so they would never have to use a
fecal bag. The food scientists couldn't create
a pill, but they came up with the next best
thing. They created foods that would make
the astronauts constipated. Those little food
cubes contained very little fiber. Fiber is the
part of food that your body can't absorb, so it
just continues traveling along your intestines,
slowly turning into poop. The less fiber you
eat, the less often you need to poop. When all
you have is a plastic bag for a bathroom, you're
happy to be constipated.

At one point, NASA food scientists tried
out a liquid diet. They figured that if astronauts
drank all their meals instead of eating them,

The first woman astronaut, Valentina Tereshkova, eating food from a tube.

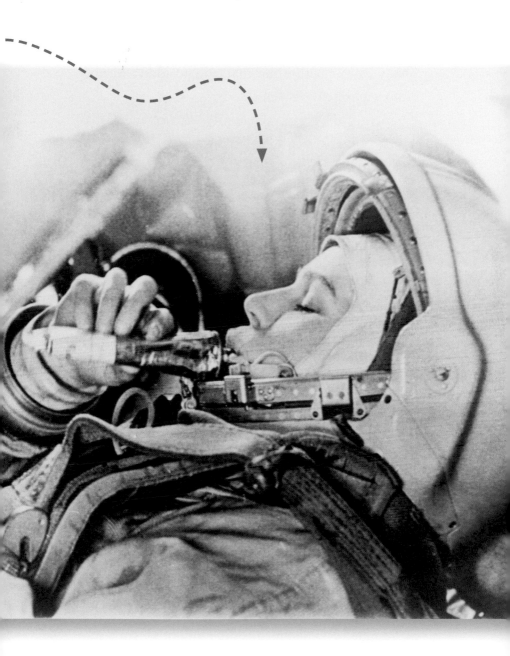

they would have "low defecation discharge frequency." That's how scientists say that you wouldn't need to poop very often.

Before they gave the liquid diet to any astronauts, NASA tested it on Earth, in a space capsule simulator. This was a pretend space capsule—really just a sealed room—where people were paid to live like astronauts while scientists studied them. The liquid diet was called the milkshake diet. What's for breakfast? Milkshake! Lunch? Another milkshake. Dinner? You guessed it! An all-milkshake diet sounds kind of great, until you try it. People on liquid diets very quickly begin to crave food they can chew. The milkshakes got even lower ratings than the cube foods. After the tests were over, one test subject admitted that he and some of the others had been dumping out portions of their meals beneath the floorboards.

Too bad you couldn't bring a charcoal grill up in space. The thing the early astronauts would have loved to eat—a steak—is a low-fiber food. Meat contains mostly just protein and fat. (Vegetables, fruits, and grains, on the other hand, have lots of fiber.) When you eat a steak, your body absorbs almost all of it. A ten-ounce sirloin steak generates only a single ounce of "residue." Residue means fiber and other stuff your body can't absorb—the stuff that ended up in the fecal bag. Eggs are also very "low-residue"—they're almost entirely protein.

That's one reason astronauts were traditionally fed steak and eggs for breakfast before they climbed aboard a space capsule to blast off. The astronauts might be stuck in their seats for hours while NASA checked everything one last time to be sure the rocket was ready to go. Astronauts wear a diaper under their space suit on launch day, but they hope they won't have to use it. Their crewmates hope so, too.

Twelve years after the corned beef sandwich incident, John Young got himself in trouble again. Young was up on the moon, sitting inside the spacecraft with his Apollo 16 crewmate Charlie Duke. The two astronauts had just finished a debriefing—a meeting by radio—with the Cap Com. Cap Com is short for "Capsule Communicator," the guy operating the radio down in NASA Mission Control. Suddenly, Young declared, "I got the farts again. I got 'em again, Charlie. I don't know what the hell gives them to me . . ."

The Cap Com came on the line to inform Young

that his microphone was still on. It's all there in the mission transcript:

Cap Com: Okay, you [have] a hot mike.

Young: Oh. How long have we had that?

Cap Com: It's been on through the debriefing.

So all the news reporters who had been listening to the debriefing—and all the people who would read their stories in the news—would know that John Young had gas.

Young blamed his attack of farts on Tang. NASA scientists doubted that Tang was the cause. They knew what did and didn't cause flatulence, because they had studied it a lot. Here's why they studied it. Flatus—the medical term for intestinal gas—is made up mostly of hydrogen and sometimes methane. These are gasses that are flammable in high concentrations—meaning they could burst into flames easily if there was a spark. A space capsule is a tiny sealed room, so any gas that you add to the air inside of it will stay there. That includes astronaut farts. NASA worried that if an astronaut contributed enough hydrogen or methane to the air inside the capsule, the concentration might get high enough that a spark could cause an explosion. They worried about it enough that the Apollo program hired a flatus expert as a consultant.

The gas in our intestines is made by the bacteria that live there. The bacteria eat the stuff we just ate. Basically, our farts are the farts of our intestinal bacteria. Everyone has different kinds and amounts of bacteria in their guts, so everyone's gas is unique. For example, about half of us don't produce methane. One scientist actually suggested that NASA keep intestinal gas in mind when it chooses new astronauts. Here's what he wrote in his report:

> The astronaut may be selected from that part of our population producing little or no methane or hydrogen and a very low level of hydrogen sulfide or other malodorous . . . flatus constituents.

Instead, NASA simply decided not to serve gassy foods. All the way through the Apollo program, beans were kept off the menu. So were foods with lots of

Modern space food: a cheeseburger wrapped in a tortilla, on the International Space Station.

sulfur compounds, like cabbage and Brussels sprouts, because they produce the gasses that make flatus stink.

Beans were put back on the menu during the space shuttle program. The space shuttle and the International Space Station are much bigger than the space capsules of Gemini and Apollo. So NASA no longer had to worry about dangerous gasses building up and causing a risk of an explosion. The astronauts could fart as much as they wanted.

Some apparently did. The no-gravity fart was rumored to be a popular pastime. Astronaut Roger Crouch told me he had heard about astronauts attempting to "launch themselves across the mid-deck." Like human rockets. Crouch was skeptical. He pointed out that people's lungs can hold more air than their rectum can, yet exhaling or sighing doesn't push an astronaut through the air.

Crouch decided to test it himself. Here's what he said to me: "In what I thought was a real voluminous and rapidly expelled [fart], I failed to move noticeably." Crouch wondered whether it might have worked better with his pants off. He did not, however, try this.

✦

Astronaut food in recent decades has begun to look more normal. Meals no longer have to be compressed or dehydrated, because there's plenty of storage room on the International Space Station. Entrees are sealed in plastic pouches and reheated in a small device that looks like a briefcase. Astronauts are allowed to eat with spoons rather than out of tubes, and they can consume things other than food that can be eaten in one bite. As long as what they're eating is thick and moist, it will stay stuck to the spoon and won't float away.

One thing astronauts still don't have up in space is fizzy soft drinks, like Coke or Mountain Dew. Without gravity, the carbonation bubbles don't rise to the surface of the can. They float all around in the liquid, and make it all weird and frothy. The Coca-Cola Company spent almost half a million dollars to develop a Coke dispenser for space. It was a waste of money, because the bubbles still caused problems. But now the problems were inside the astronauts' stomachs. Normally, in Earth gravity, bubbles rise to the top of the stomach and create a pocket of gas—otherwise known as a burp. Without gravity, the bubbles didn't rise to the top of the stomach. So the astronauts had trouble burping out the gas. They felt bloated. And when they did manage a belch, liquid often sprayed out with it. Rude!

Are you getting the idea that life in space is kind of nasty? It certainly could be. Especially in the beginning. Because the other thing astronauts didn't have? And still don't have? A shower.

Astronauts
Jim Lovell and
Frank Borman
return to Earth after
two weeks without
bathing.

6

LIFE WITHOUT A BATH

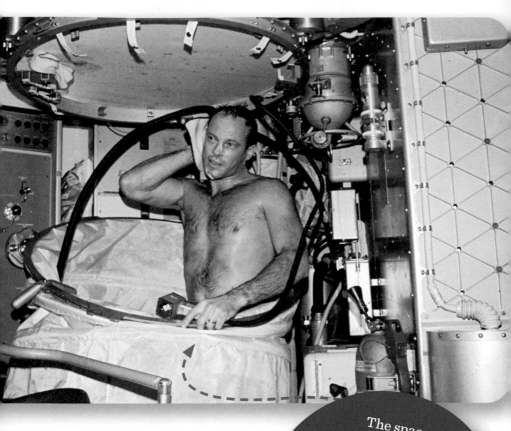

The space shower aboard Skylab. To keep the water from floating away, the curtain was pulled up to the ceiling and a vacuum system sucked the water down from the showerhead.

A trip to the moon and back could take almost two weeks. Before the Apollo moon missions began, no astronaut had ever spent so much time being weightless in space. To be sure nothing strange or dangerous would start happening to the astronauts' bodies, NASA decided to do some medical tests closer to home—up in space, but not that far away.

The tests were done during the Gemini 7 mission, in 1965. Jim Lovell and Frank Borman spent two weeks circling Earth in a space capsule while a doctor—called the flight surgeon—monitored their health. Every day, the flight surgeon got on the radio and asked them all kinds of medical questions.

Quite a few of the questions were about the astronauts' skin. For the whole two weeks of Gemini 7, Frank Borman and Jim Lovell had no way to bathe. Or shower or shampoo. Plus, they'd be sleeping in their space suits, and never taking them off. That was a safety requirement. If air began to leak out of the space capsule, the astronauts could quickly inflate their space suits and stay safe inside them while they fixed the leak. Inside their space suits, they wore "long johns"—long underwear tops and bottoms. They would be wearing that same underwear all fourteen days. And as we know from chapter 4, their toilet situation was pretty messy.

The flight surgeon asked so many skin questions that Frank Borman got tired of talking about it. Many of the Apollo astronauts had been test pilots of super-fast Air Force jets before they became astronauts. They risked their lives flying faster and higher than anyone had flown before. They didn't give a lot of thought to skin care. Here is Frank Borman, trying to ignore the questions during one of the Gemini 7 medical debriefings:

> **Mission Control:** Have you been sweating at all, Frank?

> **Borman:** [silence]

> **Mission Control:** Gemini 7 . . . Did you copy?

> **Borman:** About sweating? I'd say, yes, I'm perspiring a little.

Mission Control: Very well. Thank you.

NASA was worried about sweat, because bacteria grow best where it's wet. Sweating inside a space suit for two weeks straight, they worried, could cause painful skin problems. For instance, folliculitis. That's an infection that happens when bacteria on your skin get inside your body-hair follicles—the tiny openings in your skin where hairs come out.

There was good reason to be concerned. In the 1960s, a Soviet space biologist did some "restricted bathing" experiments. Day after day, he counted the bacteria on the skin of a group of test subjects who stopped bathing. He compared the total with the total number of bacteria on the skin of people who bathed regularly. The study subjects spent much of their day sitting in armchairs, to match the daily activity—or lack of activity—of an astronaut inside a space capsule. By around the second week of not bathing, the men in the armchairs had three times as many bacteria on their skin. On their feet and buttocks, there were up to twelve times as many bacteria. Five out of six of the men who sat around without bathing for thirty days ended up getting folliculitis. Three of them developed boils, which are especially large, swollen, painful follicle infections.

But the astronauts of Gemini 7 got neither folliculitis nor boils. "The difference is zero G," Jim Lovell told me. Because astronauts are weightless, they don't really *sit* in a seat. They float just above it. And their arms drift out to their sides, away from their body. So they're much less likely to suffer from the kind of problems normally caused by damp, dirty clothes rubbing and chafing on unwashed, sweaty skin. Thanks to weightlessness, the Gemini 7 astronauts' dirty long johns didn't stick to their buttocks and the backs of their thighs. And whatever bacteria was growing on their skin wasn't getting smushed into their follicles.

The space scientists also studied body odor. They wanted to know: How bad would it get? To find out, U.S. space biologists also did some "restricted bathing" experiments. Theirs took place at the Aerospace Medical Research Laboratories, in Ohio. This lab included a space capsule simulator—a small aluminum room where local college students could earn some cash by living like astronauts and being studied by doctors. Remember the milkshake diet and the food cubes? Those were tested in the Ohio space capsule simulator.

From January 1964 to November 1965, nine experiments on "minimal personal hygiene" took place in the space capsule simulator. Here's what the scientists meant by "minimal personal hygiene":

> No bathing or sponging of the body, no shaving, no hair and nail grooming . . . no changing clothes . . . substandard oral hygiene, and minimal use of wipes.

One team of subjects was expected to live and sleep in space suits and helmets for four weeks. Scientists thought that was what astronauts would soon be doing. But the test subjects barely made it through one day. Here's how the report put it: "Subject C became so nauseated by body odor that he was forced to remove his helmet after wearing it for less than ten hours." Subject B also took off his helmet. It didn't really help, because with the helmet removed, the men's body odors would waft out of the neck of the space suit and up into their nose when they moved or changed position. On day four, Subject B described the situation as "absolutely horrible."

So scientists had a pretty vivid idea of what Gemini 7 was going to smell like. And in fact, the reality was pretty close. In the mission transcript for the second day of Gemini 7, Borman jokingly asks

Volunteers leaving a space capsule simulator after a "minimal personal hygiene" experiment.

his crewmate Jim Lovell if he has a clothespin. "For your nose," he explains. Because Borman was about to unzip his space suit.

Making matters worse, Borman and Lovell were testing a new NASA "urine management system"—which didn't manage urine very well. It "leaked considerably," Lovell told me.

On the second day of Gemini 7, Lovell reported to Mission Control that he was about to eject a bag of urine outside the capsule, into space. (Without a toilet, this was how the astronauts got rid of their pee.) The flight surgeon asked Lovell how much urine there was, because the medical team was keeping track. "Not too much of it," Lovell replied. "Most of it's in my underwear."

I asked Lovell if he could recall the comments made by the SCUBA divers who first opened the hatch of the space capsule after it splash-landed in the ocean at the end of a space flight. "They'd get a whiff of the inside of that spacecraft and it smelled"— Lovell paused while he thought about how to say it—"different than the fresh ocean breezes outside."

Luckily, Lovell and Borman probably couldn't smell themselves anymore. If a person is exposed to a smell day after day, they "acclimate" to it. That means their brain stops letting them know about it. Smells can be a warning that something dangerous may be close by. For instance, the smell of smoke warns you that something near you may be on fire. If a smell is around all the time, your brain eventually decides that it's not a danger and stops sending the message through. Unfortunately, it takes a while to reach this point. For a group of test subjects in a twenty-day restricted-bathing Apollo space flight simulation, it wasn't until the eighth day that they acclimated and stopped being able to smell each other's body odor.

✦

Astronauts would probably agree that the worst part of not being able to bathe is not how you smell but how you feel. When you don't shower or bathe, the skin's natural oils—called "sebum"—build up on your skin. The sebum-producing glands of an adult human crank out about a teaspoon of oil onto the skin every day. This oil mixes with all the skin cells you naturally shed each day—called "dander." If you can't wash all this stuff off, you soon start to feel grubby.

The glands that secrete sebum are attached to hair follicles. That's why scalps get especially greasy when you don't bathe or shower. Like sweat, sebum develops a distinctive smell as bacteria break it down. "At least two of the Skylab astronauts reported that their heads developed offensive odors," wrote a scientist in one NASA report.

The Soviet space scientists actually measured the buildup of sebum on the skin of a group of test subjects who had stopped bathing. For the first week, the scientists discovered, the skin's oiliness stayed about the same. This was unexpected. Why didn't their skin become greasier as the days went by? Because their clothes kept absorbing the sebum and also their sweat. At the end of the experiment, the scientists had the test subjects take off their clothes and get into a bathtub. Meanwhile, their clothes went into a washtub. The scientists measured and compared the amounts of grease, sweat, and dander in the two tubs. Around 90 percent of it was in the water where the clothing had been. Only about 10 percent came off the men's bodies. This is why it's a good idea to wash your clothes every now and then.

The astronauts of Gemini 7 and the pretend astronauts in the Ohio space capsule simulator could not wash their underclothes. The report about the space capsule simulator experiment says that the subjects' clothes became so greasy and sweaty that they began sticking to their skin and becoming "very odorous" and literally starting to rot and fall apart. The situation was described as "very troublesome." Jim Lovell told me that the Gemini 7 long johns, too, were in bad shape by the end of the two-week mission. "They were," he recalled, "pretty smudged around the crotch area."

At a certain point, the fabric of a person's clothes or underwear has absorbed all the sweat and sebum it can hold. The fabric has become "saturated." After that point, the grease starts to build up on the person's skin. The Soviet researchers, who had been measuring the amount of oil on the test subjects' chests and backs, found that it takes five to seven days to reach that point. No one was measuring the oil on the skin of the Gemini 7 astronauts, but on day ten, they told the flight surgeon they were "starting to itch" and "getting a little crummy." Here they are on day twelve:

> **Mission Control:** Gemini 7, this is Surgeon. Frank, do you have any lotion remaining?

> **Borman:** Any lotion?

> **Mission Control:** Roger.

> **Borman:** We have some but we sure don't need it, Jack. We are as greasy as can be.

Once a person's clothes become saturated and oil starts building up on the skin, what happens then? Does unwashed skin get greasier and greasier forever until the person takes a bath? It does not. After five to seven days, the sebaceous glands stop pumping out sebum. Only when the person changes her shirt or takes a shower do the glands get to work again. This tells us that human skin likes to have a protective layer of oil. Skin seems to be A-OK with a week's buildup of sebum.

But people are not. That includes astronauts. In space, being able to take a bath or a shower is important for morale—for keeping the astronauts' spirits up. Without a shower or bath, astronauts start to get grumpy. They may stop caring about their work. Space agencies realized this. They spent a lot of time and money trying to develop a zero-gravity shower—especially for astronauts on the early space stations. Space station missions were longer than those of Gemini and Apollo missions. They lasted months, not weeks. And there was room on board for exercise equipment, so astronauts were sweating a lot more, in addition to getting greasy.

Of course, a normal shower wouldn't work. Earth showers depend on gravity. Without gravity, the water comes out a few inches, but it doesn't separate from the showerhead. Instead of raining down onto the astronaut, it collects in an expanding blob. This is fascinating to watch, but not very helpful if you're trying to get clean. If the astronaut held the showerhead close enough to his body to prevent the blob from forming, the water would bounce off and form smaller blobs that floated around the spacecraft. He then had to spend ten minutes chasing and capturing them.

Instead of a shower, NASA once tested a "shower suit." The plan was that the astronaut would be cleaned, rinsed, and dried while he was inside the suit, so no water blobs could escape. Unfortunately, it didn't clean very well. Or rinse very well, or dry very well.

For Skylab, NASA installed a collapsible shower that astronauts would pull up around their body. "It turned out to be easier just to forget the whole thing," said astronaut Alan Bean, when asked about it.

The shower on the Soviet space station Salyut used airflow to try to pull the water down toward the cosmonauts' feet. This didn't work very well, either. The airflow was not strong enough to overcome surface tension, so water blobs clung to the cosmonauts' bodies. They especially clung to the body's openings—like the eyes and mouth and nostrils. To keep from inhaling water and choking, the cosmonauts on the Salyut 7 mission wore snorkeling gear. "What an exotic sight it was," one of them wrote in his diary. "A naked man [flying] across the station . . . with snorkel in his mouth, goggles over his eyes, a clip on his nose." Understandably, the crew of Salyut 7 showered just once a month.

By now, the space agencies have given up on space showers. Astronauts clean themselves with moist wipes and rinseless shampoo. Japanese astronauts have something extra: self-cleaning underwear! "J-Wear" was developed at a university in Tokyo. It is made of a special high-tech fabric. Astronaut Wakata Koichi wore the same pair of J-Wear underpants for twenty-eight days without complaint.

Day six of Gemini 7. Frank Borman is on the radio with Mission Control. The conversation is moving along in the usual technical, stick-to-the-point manner of most pilot-to-ground radio communications. Until:

> **Mission Control:** Stand by for the
> Surgeon, Gemini 7.

Borman: [silence]

Mission Control: Gemini 7, this is Surgeon. Have you had any dandruff problem up there, Frank?

Borman. No.

Mission Control: Say again?

Borman: N. O. No, negative!

Borman really and truly did not wish to discuss personal hygiene. But flaking, itchy skin was a common complaint among astronauts. When you don't shower or shampoo, all the skin cells that you would normally shed and shower off each day get clumped together in your sebum. Dander plus sebum equals flakes. Plus, the air inside a spacecraft is very dry, which makes the situation worse. The early astronauts had a word for the flaking and itching of skin in space. They called it "creeps."

A blob of water floating in zero gravity.

Remember the restricted hygiene experiments in the space cabin simulator? At the end of one such experiment, according to a report, "a fine layer of powdery scales was found to cover the floor . . ." In a real spacecraft, without gravity, those scales—or skin flakes—would not fall to the floor. They'd float in the air. I asked Lovell about this. I believe my exact words were: "Was it just like a snow globe in there?" He said he didn't recall that. Then he said, "You're investigating a rather unusual aspect of space flight."

The plan for Gemini 7 was that the astronauts would keep their space suits on for the entire two weeks. But by day two, Borman and Lovell were already extremely uncomfortable. They were hot and sweaty, and the suits made it hard to move in the cramped space of the Gemini capsule. The flight surgeon took pity on them. He spoke to his bosses at NASA. They agreed to let one astronaut at a time take off his space suit and do his work wearing just his long johns. For years, Jim Lovell told me, his son would tell his friends, "Dad orbited the Earth in his underwear!"

The hardest thing about Gemini 7 probably

Astronaut Karen Nyberg washing her hair with no-rinse shampoo.

wasn't the fact that you couldn't take a shower or use a toilet or eat a big, sloppy deli sandwich. The hardest part of it was being stuck in a tiny space, day and night, with just one other person. I asked Jim Lovell what that was like. Was it a trial to spend two weeks locked in a tiny metal room with Frank Borman? He thought about it for a moment and laughed. "Two weeks with Frank Borman *anywhere* was a trial!"

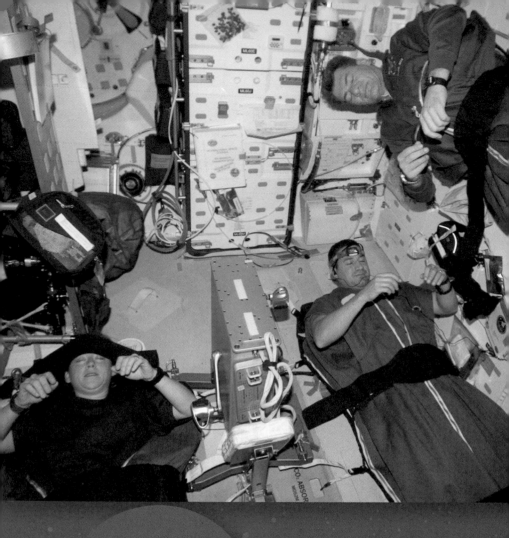

Lack of privacy: astronauts sleeping on board the space shuttle.

7

ROOMMATES FOR VERY SMALL ROOMS

Aleksandr Laveikin and Yuri Romanenko spent six months with just each other for company aboard the space station Mir in 1987.

The Soviet space station Mir looked pretty roomy from the outside. It was as big as a nine-floor apartment building laid on its side. But for the cosmonauts who lived inside it for months at a time, it didn't feel roomy at all. The part where they lived and spent most of their time—the "core module"—was the size of a small studio apartment. Each man's sleeping chamber was smaller than an airplane bathroom, and it had no door for privacy. In 1987, cosmonauts Aleksandr Laveikin and Yuri Romanenko spent six months together on Mir. After the first few months, the situation became extremely tense. Laveikin was so stressed out that he started to have heart problems and returned to Earth four months early.

I spent some time inside the replica of the Mir module inside a museum in Moscow. It was easy to imagine how being stuck in a space that small, for that long, could set two people against each other. It isn't just the size of a spacecraft's living area that is the problem. It's also the fact that you cannot leave—

because it's extremely dangerous outside. This is true of a spacecraft in space, and it's also true of a tent or cabin in an extremely harsh, deadly cold place, like Antarctica.

Or Siberia, said Romanenko. Siberia is in the Russian Arctic. Romanenko said that hunters who go to Siberia often stay there for half a year, and even though it's very lonely, they prefer to go on their own. "With only a dog for company," he said. "Because if there are two or three of you go, there will be conflict."

To learn about the psychological problems that develop on a long space voyage, psychologists sometimes study scientists who are isolated together in small buildings or tent camps in Antarctica. One thing the psychologists have discovered is that after about six weeks of being stuck with another person in a small space, you begin to find that person extremely annoying. The psychologists call this "irrational antagonism," because there is no rational reason for the hostility. One space psychology research paper included a good example of how these feelings progress. The example is from the diary of a scientist who spent four months in the Arctic with one other person, a man named Gibson. It was just the two of them, day in and day out:

I liked Gibson as soon as I saw him,
and from the moment of my arrival
we got on astonishingly well. He was
a man of poise and order, he took life
calmly. . . . But as winter closed in
around us, and week after week our
world narrowed until it was reduced
to the dimensions of a trap . . . I
began to rage inwardly and the very
traits . . . which in the beginning had
struck me as admirable, ultimately
seemed to me detestable. The time
came when I could no longer bear
the sight of this man. . . . That calm
which I had once admired I now
called laziness. . , , The meticulous
organization of his existence was
maniacal old-manliness. I could have
murdered him.

It's frustrating to be stuck in a place you don't
always want to be. In space, you can't go for a walk
or go play basketball or go shopping or do any of
the things people on Earth might do to forget their
troubles and feel better. If you're stuck long enough,

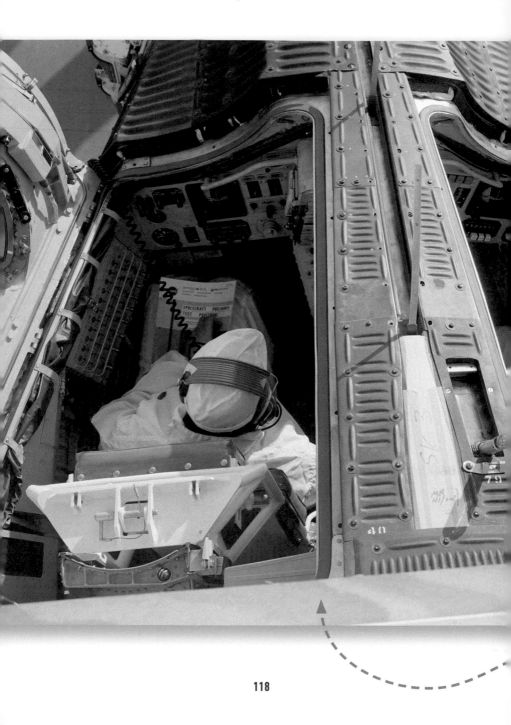

your frustration turns to anger. When you are angry, you tend to vent—to lash out at someone. An astronaut has only two kinds of people he can lash out at: a member of his crew or the person on the microphone down at Mission Control. Jim Lovell told me that astronauts try very hard not to take out their frustrations on other members of their crew. "Because you're in a risky business," he said, "and you depend on each other to stay alive."

Instead, you take it out on the people down at Mission

A tight squeeze: inside the Gemini space capsule.

Control. Psychologists call this "displacement." You lash out at someone who did nothing to cause or deserve it. Lovell seemed to do most of his displacing on the Gemini 7 nutritionist, whose name was Dr. Chance. "Note to Dr. Chance," says Lovell to Mission Control at one point in the mission transcript. "It looks like we're in a snowstorm with crumbs from the beef sandwiches. At 300 dollars a meal! I think you can do better than this." Seven hours later, Lovell gets back on the microphone: "Another memo to Dr. Chance: Chicken with vegetables, Serial Number FC680, neck is almost sealed shut. You can't even squeeze it out . . ." And a few moments later: "Continuing same memo to Dr. Chance: Just opened the seals; chicken with vegetables all over window at this time."

Laveikin and Romanenko, too, aimed their frustration and anger at Mission Control. "People who prepared tasks for us, they have no idea what on-board is like," Romanenko recalls. "Say you are running something and somebody gives you an order to switch on something else. They don't understand it's over on the other side, and I can't leave what I do here and go there." (To avoid this, space agencies tend to use astronauts as communicators. Other astronauts understand, because they've been there themselves.)

The third option is to turn one's anger inward. The result is familiar to any psychologist who deals with isolated, confined people: depression. Laveikin confided to me that there were moments when he was extremely down. "I wanted to hang myself." He shrugged. "Of course, it's impossible, because of weightlessness."

While he was on Mir, cosmonaut Romanenko wrote songs to relax. Laveikin had one of them on the computer in his office, and he offered to play it for me. An interpreter translated the lyrics for me: "Earth, we say goodbye to you. . . . But the time will come when we will drop into the blueness of the dawn, like a morning star." And then the chorus: "I will fall into the grass and fill my lungs with air. / I will drink water from the river. / I will kiss the ground, I will hug my friends . . ." The interpreter wiped away a tear.

People can't anticipate how much they'll miss nature until they are deprived of it. I have read about submarine crews who hang around the sonar room, listening to whale songs and colonies of snapping shrimp. Or they ask to look through the periscope, just to see the clouds or catch a glimpse of a seabird.

Astronauts who had no prior interest in gardening spend their free time inside experimental greenhouses. "They are our love," said one cosmonaut, referring to the tiny flax plants they were growing on Salyut 1, the first Soviet space station.

Romanenko talked about how much he missed the smells of Earth. "Can you imagine being even one week in a locked car? Smell of metal. Smell of paint, rubber."

Laveikin says his stay on Mir was a hundred times harder than what he had expected. "It's hard work, dirty work. Very noisy, very hot." He had motion sickness for more than a week. He recalls turning to Romanenko during the first few days, saying, "And we will stay here for *half year?*"

I asked a NASA space psychologist if he thought being an astronaut was the best job in the world or the worst job in the world. Here's how he answered: "You're sleep-deprived, and you have to perform perfectly or else you don't fly anymore. As soon you're done with something, ground control is telling you something else to do. The bathroom stinks, and you have noise all the time. You can't open a window. You can't go home, you can't be with your family, you can't relax. And you're not well paid. Can you get a worse job than that?"

I don't think most astronauts feel that way. They became astronauts because they dreamed of exploring space and traveling to places no human has ever been. They'd happily sign up for a trip to Mars, even a one-way trip. To some people, a one-way voyage to Mars sounds like exile—a prison sentence in a barren land. For others, it's a chance to make history and advance scientific discovery and progress. It's a bold adventure in a world no human can even imagine.

Astronauts Robert Behnken and Douglas Hurley aboard SpaceX's Dragon capsule, 2020.

CONCLUSION

As we've seen, living in space is more challenging and a lot less comfortable than living on Earth. With NASA and SpaceX making plans to send people to Mars, it looks like we may be doing a lot more of it in the coming decades.

The planet Mars is hundreds of times farther away than the moon. It took the Apollo astronauts only a few days to arrive on the moon. The trip to Mars will take about seven months. That's a very long time to be stuck with your roommates in a small metal space with no shower or pizza delivery or family vacations.

Going to Mars is also more dangerous. The more time astronauts spend in space, the more time their bodies are exposed to dangerous radiation that zips around in space. And because they're floating around in their spaceship home instead of walking, the bones and muscles of their legs start to get weak. To prevent this, astronauts have to spend around *two hours a day* working out on exercise machines.

And a trip to Mars is a lot more expensive. Sending

astronauts to Mars will cost hundreds of billions of dollars. How do we justify the cost and risk? What good will come of it, especially when robotic landers can do much of the science just as well, if not as fast? Is this something we should do?

If you ask NASA, they will give you a long list of important technologies that have resulted from aerospace innovations over the decades. It's pretty impressive: high-speed wireless data transfer and solar panels; better artificial limbs, implantable heart monitors, and computerized insulin pumps. Look around at the items in your home. If you see something cordless or fireproof, lightweight and strong, miniaturized or automated, chances are good that the space program had a hand in the technology. Dustbusters! Bicycle helmets! Flat-screen TVs!

But there are better reasons than that, I believe. Remember the Montgolfier brothers and their hot-air balloons—from the first chapter of this book? It was the late 1700s, and it was the first time humans had dared to travel high into the air. Someone from a newspaper asked Benjamin Franklin what use there could possibly be for such a thing. "What use," he replied, "is a newborn baby?" What Franklin meant was that air travel was in its infancy. Just as a baby could grow up to discover the cure for cancer, a commitment to space travel could mean a future for humans on other planets. It began with a colorful balloon, but today we have five-hour jet flights to Europe and space probes that travel three billion miles to Pluto. If we keep on exploring, keep traveling farther, who knows where things will end up. Who knows what strange wonders that future may hold. To explore space is to keep the door open to that future.

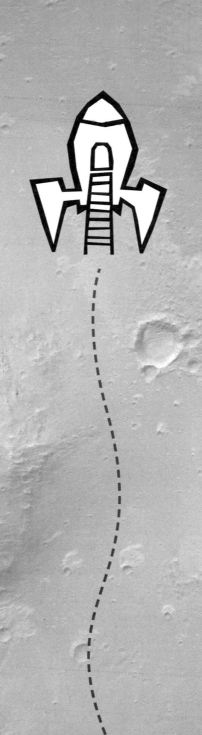

Acknowledgments

Initial outings in a new genre are often a lurching, trying affair that lands far shy of the mark. This book was, amazingly, free of all that, and I have Simon Boughton to thank. His unerring ear and instincts are always on point, and he is a joy to work with. I was extremely fortunate that Steph Romeo was available to help with the photo selections and permissions, and that the amazing Janet Byrne was on hand to copyedit. All three are, truly, as good as it gets. Finally, I want to extend my gratitude to my longtime editor and friend Jill Bialosky, who encouraged me to undertake the project and helped guide it to its finished state.

Index

Pages in *italics* refer to photographs.

Picture Credits

Pages viii–ix: NASA; p. 2: NASA/JPL-Caltech; p. 5: NASA; pp. 6–7: NASA; p. 8: US Army; p. 10: North Wind Picture Archives/Alamy Stock Photo; pp. 16–17: NASA; pp. 20–21: NASA; p 22: NASA; pp. 26–27: NASA; p. 30: NASA; pp. 34–35: NASA; p. 36: NASA; p. 43: Naval Medical Research Unit (NAMRU) – Dayton; p. 44: NASA; pp. 48–49: NASA; p. 51: NASA; p. 54: NASA; p. 56: NASA; p. 67: © 2006 SAE International https://doi.org/10.4271/2006-01-2180; p. 68: NASA; pp. 70–71: NASA; pp. 72–73; p. 74: NASA; p. 80: Smithsonian Air & Space Museum; pp. 82–83: Everett Collection Historical/Alamy Stock Photo; pp. 88–89: NASA; pp. 92–93: Time Life Pictures/NASA/The LIFE Picture Collection via Getty Images; p. 94: NASA; p. 100: Air Force Research Laboratory; pp. 108–9: NASA; p. 111: NASA; pp. 112–13: NASA; p. 114: Sputnik/Alamy Stock Photo; pp. 118–19: NASA; pp. 124–25: NASA; p. 126: NASA/JPL-Caltech.